RECLAIMING YOUR KINGSHIP

By Oscar Jones

Reclaiming Your Kingship
Copyright ©2024 Oscar Jones
ISBN: 978-1-963020-00-7

Cover design Kingdom Graphic Design
Published by Destiny House Publishing, LLC

All rights reserved.

No part of this book may be reproduced or transmitted in any form or by any means: electronic, mechanical, including photocopying and recording, or by any information storage and retrieval system, without permission in writing from the publisher.

Printed in the United States of America

Unless otherwise stated, all scripture quotations are from the Holy Bible, King James Version. Scripture references that do not have the Bible version noted are the author's paraphrase.

For more information:

Destiny House Publishing, LLC
www.destinyhousepublishing.com
email: inquiry@destinyhousepublishing.com
P.O. Box 19774
Detroit, MI 48219
888-890-9455

Acknowledgments & Dedications

I acknowledge the King of all kings, my Lord and Savior Jesus Christ who has made me a king and priest. Thank you for your love, faithfulness, and lavish.

I acknowledge my wife, Crystal Jones. She is my rock, inspiration and encourager. Her belief in me helped me to get over the finish line. Thank you sweetheart for all your support.

I dedicate this book to my two sons who are young kings, Jake Antonio Allen and Christopher Michael Jones. You are my heritage. I appreciate the great men that you are. I know God will grace you to come into the full revelation of who you are and that you will pass it on to your young princes.

I also dedicate this book to my sons in the gospel, Tony Winans, Ralph Williams and Nick Bonhomme who are living to serve God as kings in the Kingdom.

TABLE OF CONTENTS

Chapter 1: What Happened? 1

Chapter 2: The Plan 9

Chapter 3: Understand Your Kingship 15

Chapter 4: Restoring the King in Me 27

Chapter 5: Creating A Kingdom Culture 35

Chapter 6: Walk With God 39

Chapter 7: Manhood, Marriage, and Ministry 45

Chapter 8: Act Like A King 51

Chapter 9: Satan: Identity Thief 61

Chapter One

What Happened?

Adam and Eve happened. They lost their dominion because they listened to the enemy. They believed the lie and acted on what God told them NOT to do. As a result, they were expelled from the garden.

Genesis 1:26-28 reads, *And God said, Let us make man in our image, after our likeness: and let them have dominion over the fish of the sea, and over the fowl of the air, and over the cattle, and over all the earth, and over every creeping thing that creepeth upon the earth. ²⁷ So God created man in his own image, in the image of God created he him; male and female created he them. ²⁸ And God blessed them, and God said unto them, Be fruitful, and multiply, and replenish the earth, and subdue it: and have dominion over the fish of the sea, and over the fowl of the air, and over every living thing that moveth upon the earth.*

God intended for mankind to govern and rule His kingdom on earth. He created a garden and put man in it to rule and guard it. God created this beautiful place for mankind. He intended that we would have dominion in the garden. Which would eventually become the world that we live in today. God's original plan was bringing his Kingdom which was in heaven to earth.

Genesis 3:1 - *Now the serpent was more subtle than any beast of the field which the Lord God had made. And he said unto the woman, Yea, hath God said, Ye shall not eat of every tree of the garden?*

Satan's plot to overthrow the kingdom of God begin with a *lie*. To overthrow God's kingdom, he needed to deceive man. The usurper came to take that which wasn't his. As a result, man lost the ability to walk in kingdom dominion with God. Man found himself hiding from God. As a result, we lost our authority and we lost our identity.

This act of ignorance cost mankind so much. We lost our identity when we subjected ourselves to the evil one. We no longer identified with God. In John 10:10, it says that Satan comes to steal. He wants to take from us that which rightly belongs to us. Our identity is one of our greatest weapons. When the devil steals our identity, he misuses it for counterfeit purposes. He violated spiritual laws and usurped our authority. He has acted in our name against God's name. He throws the rock and hides his hand.

Today, he tells you that you are not who God says that you are. You can find yourself caught up in a web of sin and lies, when you give audience to Satan. He means us no good.

Identity theft thwarts purpose. Vision and focus are lost. Without a vision, we know the people perish. You are left holding onto a *perceived* identity or the way you want others to see you. You can't thrive and do all that God has purposed for you unless you are moving in your true identity. True identity helps you to understand the assignment. My assignment is to help others see who they are. That is how I help expand the kingdom.

> *If you never recover your identity, you will never understand your purpose.*

However if a person has a stolen identity, he defines himself by what he does. If he messed up, he is a mess. If he told a lie, he is a liar. If he falls into fornication, he is a fornicator. And the list goes on. When the enemy is able to steal, he fogs your vision. You become unsure of yourself.

Insecurity can be debilitating. It will only allow you to go so far. You will have limited ability and potential. You lack boldness and courage to do what you were designed to do.

You become disabled all because you can't identify yourself. And you have a ton of blotches or accusations on your record. These accusations come from the wicked one. He is the accuser of the brethren.

But whose report will you believe? Because the word tells me in Romans 8:17 that I am a child of God and if I am a child of God than I am an heir of God and a joint heir with Christ.

I also recognize my position as a king in God's kingdom. I Peter 2:9 says that we are a chosen generation, a royal priesthood, and a holy nation, and a peculiar or (special) people that we should show forth the praises of Him who called us of darkness.

As you begin your own discovery for identity, ask yourself, who am I in Christ? What is my purpose? And how does God want to use me? These nagging questions demand answers.

There is the tendency to find the answers by our own methods. The spirit of man is searching for something, unaware that we are trying to get back to the garden. We are frantically searching for life's meaning. As our quest goes on, we often try to find answers in substances, religion, recreation, or work. Either of these will satisfy you for a season; but all will eventually leave you completely empty and frustrated.

The very nature of the search means something you once possessed is missing. How can I long for something I never had.

All of us have wondered about the meaning of life. A child asks his parents, "Why was I born?" Something in their little soul tells them something is missing. We miss being with our Father.

Roman 5:12 *Therefore, just as sin entered the world through one man, and death through sin, so also death was passed on to all men, because all sinned.*

1 Corinthians 15:22 *For as in Adam all die, even so in Christ shall all be made alive.*

Sin came in and separated us from God, physically and spiritually. We lost our fellowship with the Father. Man began to live without God. Sin took root in our hearts and man lived out his life in the natural realm. Jeremiah 17:9 *The heart is deceitful and desperately wicked who can know it.*

But I thank God that He put something in us that sin could not touch, that is the longing to be with Him.

We all crave to return to our original destiny to be one with our God in His kingdom. It is in the very fiber of our being to yearn to be with Him. You may have heard sermons about that hole in your heart that only God can fill. It is real. It is that spiritual DNA that connect us to our Father. We didn't lose it in the garden. Our desire to be with the Father remains. Sin has usurped the authority that God gave us in the garden, but it wasn't able to touch the longing of our human hearts.

Satan has always tried to be like God. He wants us to worship him. He tries to use our longing for God to get us into other things. Addictions, control, lust, and all kinds of perversions.

But God is able to satisfy the longing of our hearts. We long to be one with our God in his kingdom.

What Happened?

The evil one is always trying to substitute what God is doing. He started with Eve, and he has not stopped trying to gain footage in our hearts.

God's kingdom is planted in the earth through us. Satan has come with his own plan to try to answer man's questions. Satan's scheme is to get the ache of the human spirit to find peace and satisfaction in anything but an authentic relationship with Jesus Christ.

God had already created us to be like him. When we live in the sin nature, we want to be like him, but apart from him. It is a trap of Satan. He, too, wants to be like God apart from Him. He continues to offer man this fruit. *"Be like me"* is really what Satan is saying. It is impossible to be like God outside of Him. It results in pain, torment, and hopelessness. You will lose peace, joy and find yourself unfulfilled.

There is a Master plan, and it is our duty to follow it. Unfortunately, when we open our eyes to sin, we will bite the fruit that Satan offers us, and our eyes close to God's plans and purposes. We are unable to see spiritually. We blindly grope around the earth doing whatever we think we want to do, hitting and missing in life.

Can you see the problem?

Fortunately, God always has an answer. We will be exploring those answers as we continue through these pages.

Chapter Two

The Plan

When a house is built, and its result does not match the blueprint, the builder has to go back to the original design to pinpoint the problem.

God's original purpose for man was altered, but this didn't surprise God. He is Alpha and Omega. He knows the end of a thing at the beginning. God hasn't changed His mind about us. He knew what was up and already had a plan to restore mankind. If intent is unknown than there will be no clarity. Therefore, if we misunderstand God's intent, that would guarantee misuse of purpose and a waste of gifts and time.

When we don't really understand God's original purpose, it creates a lot of chaos in our lives.

Misunderstanding God's purposes creates an identity crisis in the souls of believers who are looking for God in all the wrong places. Therefore, it is imperative that we understand intent before we can understand our kingship.

If we don't understand who God is and why we are here, then restoring our authority will be pointless. Mark 1:15 reads, The time is fulfilled, and the kingdom of God is at hand: repent ye, and believe the gospel.

Jesus said it is time for the God's plan to come to fruition. It's time for the kingdom of God to reign here on earth. This is the heart of God.

In order for that to happen, we must turn from our way of thinking.

That means repentance is in order. The word repent means to change your mind. It mean to turn around literally and walk circumspectly.

2 Corinthian 7:9-11

[9] Now I rejoice, not that ye were made sorry, but that ye sorrowed to repentance: for ye were made sorry after a godly manner, that ye might receive damage by us in nothing.

[10] For godly sorrow worketh repentance to salvation not to be repented of: but the sorrow of the world worketh death.

^{11} For behold this selfsame thing, that ye sorrowed after a godly sort, what carefulness it wrought in you, yea, what clearing of yourselves, yea, what indignation, yea, what fear, yea, what vehement desire, yea, what zeal, yea, what revenge! In all things ye have approved yourselves to be clear in this matter.

Repentance is a particularly important part of God's plan.

Paul gives us here an example of what Godly repentance looks like in 2 Corinthians 7:9 -11. There are seven fruits of Godly repentance that he talks about that gives us an idea of what repentance looks like.

> *Without godly repentance, there can be no restoration or reconciliation to walk within the kingdom.*

Seven Fruits of Godly Repentance

He said what carefulness it brought in you.

1. **Carefulness** is about becoming cautious about sin or the issues that caused us to fall. We become vigilant about what we watch, what we hear, what we see in other words we are very careful about the things that offend God. What carefulness it wrought in you.

2. What **clearing of yourselves** means that you have to go back and adjust to make sure that the matter has been cleared. It means to apologize or to make it right. To free oneself from blame and to remove evil from one's midst.

3. What **indignation** - you become righteously angry about that thing. Anger is not about self-pity or regret. It is fiery hatred against sin.

4. What **fear** – this is the fear that this thing would be repeated. The fear of the Lord is the beginning of wisdom, *and* the fear of the Lord shall make you clean. There is a reverential fear that is due towards God. If you were a fornicator and you really repent of that thing there's a fear that comes over you when the temptation of those things try to reappear. There is a reverential fear and respect towards God that gives you wisdom and keeps you clean.

5. What **zeal** – Repentant people have zeal. They become advocates for righteousness in that sin area. When I went out on my marriage (many years ago) and committed adultery, I repented of that thing and God restored me. There was a zeal that was created in me. For example, my wife and I begin to teach and help others through their

issues of adultery. Zeal is created in us when we have a godly repentance for a thing.

6. The **vehement desire** is a passionate and intense desire to please God. This passion is the fuel that drives you to righteousness. Your earnest desire is to please God.

7. And lastly, the fruits of godly repentance bring **revenge**. Revenge is not against a person because vengeance belongs to God. It is a desire for justice.

God's plan was to restore our authority as kings back to us as we live in his kingdom here on earth. We are kings in His kingdom, with the power to execute his will. So, thank you Jesus, He doesn't leave us in that sinful state. God's plan was for us to rule and have dominion over the earth and everything in it.

The grace of God is both redemptive and empowering. Not only does God's grace give us access into Heaven, but it also qualifies us to rule here on Earth as well. The same grace that redeems you carries within it the empowerment you need for every part of your life.

Ephesians 2:8 *For by grace you have been saved through faith, and that not of yourselves; it is the gift of God.*

'*Sozo*' is the Greek word for saved. It means redemption as well as wholeness, healing, prosperity, restoration, and victory.

All of this comes to us as a result of salvation. As believers, we now have authority to reign in our marriages, ministries, and careers and to live a life that glorifies God. As a result of this grace, you are no longer a victim of sin, sickness, oppression, poverty, or other negative circumstances; instead you now have authority over the devil and his agents. This authority to reign is not based on our family background or social status; it is our spiritual birth right as citizens.

Our mission is to do His will. God never intended to build a garden and leave it empty. From the beginning God's plan was to fill the earth with His righteousness. The whole earth shall be filled with His glory. The earth is the Lord and the fullness thereof.

When we understand our kingship it will cause us to take our rightful place in the kingdom. Then we can be those instruments of change in the hand of God to expand His invisible heavenly kingdom in the Earth realm.

Chapter Three
Understanding your Kingship

*E*xodus 19:5-6 *Now therefore, I keep my covenant, then ye shall be a peculiar treasure unto me above all people: for all the earth is mine: And you shall be unto me a kingdom of priests, and an holy nation. These are the words which thou shalt speak unto the children of Israel.*

Rev 1:6 *And hath made us kings and priests unto God and His Father.*

Rev 5:10 *And hast made us unto our God kings and priests and we shall reign on the earth." And you shall be unto Me a kingdom of priests and a Holy nation"*

(Ex. 19:6) Every believer is both a king and a priest, a "royal priest". A king has authority, a priest has access. We have both.

We have the ministry of kings and priests. Kings, in the old days, did battle with the world's system and took the resources and shared with God's priests, so the priests could focus on nurturing a moral and godly people. The priests offered sacrifices to God on behalf of the kings before battle. It was a God inspired partnership. That's why Saul got in trouble; He offered the sacrifice that the kings were not supposed to offer. It was the job of the priests. He overstepped his bounds.

But today, the King of all kings grants us authority to live as kings. We are children of God, and if children, then heirs; heirs of God and joint heirs with Christ. So that we have the authority to use the name of Jesus. We are kings in the kingdom. As a result, we have authority to change situations in His name and to bring people into the kingdom.

Matthew 28:18-20 *And Jesus came and spoke to them, saying, "All authority has been given to Me in heaven and on earth. {19} "Go therefore and make disciples of all the nations, baptizing them in the name of the Father and of the Son and of the Holy Spirit, {20} "teaching them to observe all things that I have commanded you; and lo, I am with you always, even to the end of the age.*

As we understand who we are, we are expected to learn how to live here on earth in a manner consistent with our royal status. We are expected to obey our King and His teachings. If you hold to my teaching, you are really my disciples" *(John 8:31)*. "If you love me, you will obey what I command" *(John 14:15)*. "If anyone loves me, he will obey my teaching" *(John 14:23)*. "Remain in me and I will remain in you," (John 15:4). "If you obey my command, you will remain in my love" *(John 15:10)*. "And this is his command: to believe in the name of his Son, Jesus Christ, and to love one another as he commanded us. Those who obey his commands live in him, and he in them. And this is how we know that he lives in us: We know it by the Spirit he gave us" *(1 John 3:23-24)*.

We can only understand our kingship by understanding the words of the King. He tells us to love one another and to obey his commands. By obeying his commands and loving one another, we work within his domain. As we operate within His kingdom, our lives begin to reflect His kingship.

It is imperative that we study to show ourselves approved, workmen rightly dividing the word of truth (II Timothy 2:15). It is foundational to us fulfilling the work of the kingdom in this lost and dying world.

Religion is a system chiefly based on rules and regulations for morality. It tries to substitute God and replace His kingdom. Religion is rigid and dry.

God calls us into relationship which supersedes religious tradition. It is a love union with the King, which offers mercy and grace to all those who embrace it.

A true king is never voted into or out of power; nor is His throne overtaken by force. He is born into power.

John 3:3 reads, *Jesus answered him, "Truly, truly, I say to you, unless one is born again[b] he cannot see the Kingdom of God".* Kingship is a birthright given to us by Jesus. We are born again into kingship. We are joined together with Christ.

Once you become a king, you remain a king. Since Christ will never die, neither will we die. But we will reign with him forever and ever.

In a kingdom, the king decides who will be citizens. We are loyal citizens of God's kingdom because the King of kings has called us His sons. Isn't that wonderful?

The welfare of the citizens is the personal responsibility of the King. In Matthew 6:25 Jesus said take no thought for your life for what you should eat or what you should put on. If he takes care of the sparrow, how much more valuable are we? We don't worry about our life as kingdom citizens. God has promised us that He's got us. When we obey the King, he is compelled to take care of us.

Christ's authority is unconditional and unlimited. It can't be changed by anyone or any governing body. No one can break his authority over our lives…but us.

By understanding Christ's authority it grants us a freedom as his royal subjects to be free to serve him. we aren't bound by sin and the things of this world that keeps us down. Because we understand that we are subject to His kingship. This may be hard to understand in these United States because we live in a democracy. When we are able to see God as the kind King and understand His loving leadership, it frees us to be obedient servants to do his will.

In the kingdom, the King owns everything. Psalm 24 reads, *the earth is the Lord's and the fullness thereof.* We as royal subjects are put here as stewardships over the King's property. God has given us all things to enjoy. When we walk in our full authority, we see situations on earth as fleeting. We don't get attached to material things. They belong to God and He can use whatever He wants to use whenever He wants to use it. We are submitted to the king.

In the animal kingdom the lion rules and he has a domain. The alpha male understands his leadership. And every subject that is in that pride comes subject to that king, the alpha lion. All the other animals in the jungle also know that the lion is king. They flee at his presence. When a lion walks within the jungle, his authority is respected.

God has given us to be kings and priests. And everything must come subject to us as mankind. We are to rule and govern the earth, as God sees fit. As I have said earlier every man has a domain. Understanding your kingship will help you understand how to rule your house, how to be a husband, how to be a father and how to lead your pride.

We are to think and act the way the King of kings thinks and acts. We must have the mind of Christ. It is in our best interest to follow and allow the Spirit of God to dwell in us. When we find ourselves acting contrary to the King, we have to repent of our selfish ways.

Jesus Christ was willing to give His life for us. We are told we must put away sin and follow Him: *"Let us lay aside every weight, and the sin which so easily ensnares us, and let us run with endurance the race that is set before us, looking unto Jesus, the author and finisher of our faith, who for the joy that was set before Him endured the cross, despising the shame, and has sat down at the right hand of the throne of God"* (Hebrews 12:1-2).

Our most important kingdom assignment is to love, and to learn to be like Jesus. We must take on the character of the King, following Him closely. Jesus said my kingdom is not of this world.

As men of God, understand that your kingship is directly related to His kingship. We must be students of His character and His word to rule in His kingdom. We must also realize that kingship isn't predicated on future events. We are kings now. Religion tries to tell us that we are to look for a future kingdom. So all of our anticipation is looking toward the future.

The danger in that is it blocks our mindsets so that we no longer look at ourselves as kings in the present. It causes us to look to the future ignoring and excusing the present.

> *If we are kings today, our behavior and attitude must change today.*

What we do today is more important than what we say we will do tomorrow. It is the present that matters the most. If I see myself as a nothing but a mere man, that is the trick of the enemy. You and I must recognize that God has called us kings and that changes everything. Who I am as a king will change who I am as a son, husband, father, and brother. I am a God's royal son.

Embracing your kingship will cause you to war against the negative mindsets of insecurity, shame, uncontrolled anger, accusations, jealousy, and a critical spirit. This will empower you to rebuke generational curses that try to attack your soul. It gives you the fuel to fight against your flesh in order to maintain your status as a king.

There is a constant war going on within your members according to Roman 7:23. As a man thinketh so is he. So understanding your kingship helps you in the battle. It gives you the ammunition to win.

Let me give you some principles concerning your kingship as we rediscover the kingdom of God in us. Jesus said the kingdom of God is within us. We have the ultimate source of authority through the authority given to us by the King.

Once we become believers of Jesus Christ and enter the kingdom of God, we surrender our citizenship

> *You are a king belonging to the King who lives inside of you.*

in this carnal world. Remember, we are in this world, but not of it. We enter the kingdom through Christ, He is the doorway. God has accepted us as kingdom citizens and empowered us to do his bidding. We command mountains to fall. We defeat demons. We call things that be not as though they already are. It is our birthright.

Regardless of where we are, whether at our place of employment, at a social function or whatever, we must remember that we are God's royal subjects. We must govern ourselves accordingly. We represent Him, (not any religious group or denomination which goes under the banner of Christianity). The authority of our government backs us up. All of the rights, privileges and benefits of our citizenship apply fully to us even though we live in a foreign land.

Remember, at any time we can call on the resources of our King. When five thousand men (not counting women and children) needed to be fed, Jesus' disciples saw only the limited resources of this world: five loaves of bread and two fish. However Jesus looked into His Father's pantry and saw enough to feed everyone and still have twelve baskets full left over. Now if that isn't God taking care of His citizens, I don't know what is.

While He was teaching the masses the concept of the kingdom, He never allowed them to want for anything while they followed Him. And that's the concept we must understand. Jesus will always take care of his citizens for He is the Good King.

In Luke 12:22 *And he said unto his disciples, Therefore I say unto you, Take no thought for your life, what ye shall eat; neither for the body, what ye shall put on. Life is more than meat, and the body is more than raiment. Consider the ravens: for they neither sow nor reap; which neither have storehouse nor barn; and God feedeth them: how much more are ye better than the fowls? And which of you with taking thought can add to his stature one cubit? If ye then be not able to do that thing which is least, why take ye thought for the rest? Consider the lilies how they grow: they toil not, they spin not; and yet I say unto you, that Solomon in all his glory was not arrayed like one of these. If then God so clothe the grass, which is to day in the field, and to morrow is cast into the oven; how much more will he clothe you, O ye of little faith? And seek not ye what ye shall eat, or what ye shall drink, neither be ye of doubtful mind. For all these things do the nations of the world seek after and your Father knoweth that ye have need of these things. But rather seek ye the Kingdom of God; and all these things shall be added unto you. Fear not, little flock; for it is your Father's good pleasure to give you the kingdom.*

God tells us to not worry about our lives, clothes, food, or anything. He asks us to not be like the Pharisees or the world who worry about these things. The King provides for us. He will supply every need. David said in Psalm 37:25, *I have been young, and now am old; Yet, I have not seen the righteous forsaken nor his descendants begging bread.*

God is very concerned about our physical needs. He wants us to trust Him to provide. Trust that He is loving and will not neglect those that are His.

As true representatives of the kingdom we must be men of compassion with love and concern for all people. We are responsible for providing for families whatever is necessary to meet their needs. When we submit to God by obeying His instruction, He will put in our hands what we need to take care of the needs of our families.

As we identify as kings in God's amazing kingdom, it should compel us to seek the King. There is always more to learn about the King in order to live righteously in His kingdom.

Rise up men of God and know who you are. Allow the King to restore in us the **_roar_** that the enemy has taken. We are the alpha males. We will do God's will starting in our marriages, families, churches and community. We are God's chosen.

Chapter Four

Restoring the King in Me

God hasn't changed His mind about you. Even with all your weaknesses and flaws, He still accepts you as a king in His kingdom.

From the moment Adam lost his kingship and was expelled from the Garden of Eden, God has been working all things after the counsel of His will to restore this world and everything in it back to Himself. We all know the sad consequences when Eve partook of the fruit, and Adam did, too. Sin entered the earth and the so did death (Romans 6:23). Adam's disobedience caused a disconnect between his spirit and the Spirit of God. Adam and Eve began to live out of their souls instead of their spirits. (Your soul is your mind, will, intellect, reasoning, imaginations and emotions.) They were led by their five senses – touch, hearing, sight, smell and taste – instead of their spirits. Before the fall, they simply knew what they needed to know. They could draw any knowledge they needed directly from God's Spirit.

The Holy Spirit is our teacher who will lead us and guide us in all truth. He is the One who is actively involved in the restitution of all things. So, the Spirit-led life is the answer to walking out your kingship. Jesus said it is the Father's good pleasure to give us the kingdom (Luke 12:32). Also scripture declares that all creation is waiting for the manifestation of the sons of God (Romans 8:19).

There is a renewal of our kingship. We must be led by the Spirit. God's spirit is the catalyst to restoration. To restore is to go back and find what was lost. God wants to restore our kingship as we walk out his promises. As I stated earlier we lost a lot, but the Spirit of God is restoring man back.

> *Restoring your position as king requires that you know who you are and who your Father is.*

You are a king created for God's glory to bring forth His kingdom in this earth realm. Gaining a healthy view of your King is essential. It will produce a healthy fear of God. This will cause our kingship to thrive by embracing a Godly fear. This kind of fear is "awe-filled respect". It is not about being afraid of God, but reverencing Him. The same respect we want from others we are to lay at the feet of our King. We must recognize His power and position and give him proper honor. It is this reverential fear of God, which is a controlling motivation in our lives. In matters both spiritually and morally, it is fear of displeasing Him. A reverential 'fear' of God will inspire a constant carefulness in dealing with the Lord and with others. We live in respect to the King.

Within a kingdom, the King's word is law. So it is in the kingdom of God, God's word is the law we live by. As we embrace this holy fear, it creates a desire for the King's word. The more we hear and obey His word, the more our minds are renewed, and our nature is changed. The renewing process is continual in our souls. Romans 12 tells us that we must renew our minds by the word of God. We must study, read, pray, and seek God for revelation knowledge.

When Jesus asked the disciples, "Who do men say that I am?" They begin to describe certain prophets and various ones of the Old Testament. But Peter said, "Thou art the Christ, the son of the living God!" Jesus told him, flesh and blood have not revealed this to you but my Father in heaven. In other words, Peter got a revelation of who Jesus was through the Holy Spirit. Restoration will come as revelation knowledge of the King is revealed in our spirits.

In churches today, often we get inspired, but inspiration will only encourage you and make you feel better about yourself or your situation, temporarily. But revelation from the spirit will change your heart and your mind towards God permanently. We need revelation in order to understand the kingdom.

Jesus told Peter that your name would no longer be called Simon, but Peter. God changed Peter's name because of the revelation that he received. It is in our revelation that we change. I believe Peter was changed because of the revelation he received at the time. Inspiration is good, but unless we get revelation we can never truly be restored in our kingship. **But God will give us revelation concerning the kingdom as we seek him to renew our minds.**

Ephesians 2:6 *God raised us up with Christ and seated us with him in the heavenly realms in Christ Jesus.*

How does that play out in our everyday lives? Do you understand what that means? Without getting a revelation it can be misinterpreted. God has set us in heavenly places. We are no longer servants. He calls us friends. In other words, when Jesus came, He tore the veil and gave us access. We can go to our King at any time. As a matter of fact, He said come boldly to the throne of grace to find help in the time of trouble. We can come to him *without* our heads hung down in shame or fear. We are His. So we can come to Him for help *whenever* we need it.

God has given us kingly authority, to bind and to loose and to speak a thing into existence. We can decree a thing and it shall be established. This type of power and authority is granted to kings.

> *WE HAVE UNLIMITED ACCESS TO THE KING.*

When Adam was in the garden, God gave him the authority to name the animals. Whatever Adam named the animal that's what it was called. It was because Adam had the authority, he walked in his kingship. Just as Adam had the authority to name animals, he had the authority to keep and to dress the garden. Today, as kingdom believers when we come to Christ, and we are restored back into our kingship we have the same authority.

Kingship is your path to a rich life full of success and significance. You were born to win. You are a king, and you were created for dominion (Genesis 1:28).

Satan doesn't want you to understand that you are a king. Because he knows the authority you have to cast him out and trample on him. You will cause him to shake in his boots. Can you picture that? You sitting as king and Satan is under your feet terrified of your holy reign. That is a real picture of your power.

Kings have the authority to occupy. Luke 19:13 says, And he called his ten servants, and delivered them ten pounds, and said unto them, Occupy till I come.

Occupy does not mean to withdraw. It means to march aggressively into another territory with spiritual force for the purpose of conquest and possession.

We are repossessing what was ours. We will regain all that was taken from us at the beginning.

God is renewing our kingship so that we can produce a kingdom culture here on earth. He wants people all over the earth to see the evidence of His kingdom in the values and lifestyle of His children and to be drawn by our influence.

Your authority comes from God to strengthen His kingdom on the earth.

Reclaiming Your Kingship

Chapter Five
Creating a Kingdom Culture

Jesus said in Matt. 16:18, that He would build his church and the gates of hell would not prevail against it. The church isn't the kingdom of God, but the church is of the kingdom and is the agent and messenger of the kingdom. The church is assigned the task of creating a kingdom culture in our local congregations, and to carry this culture into society to bring heaven's influence.

We must remember that the kingdom of God is already here. The kingdom compels the church to walk in the fullness of what is available to us now, not later on.

Creating a kingdom culture here on earth begins in our families. God created the family first, and he wants us to create that culture in our homes before we can reach out into the world.

Within the context of scripture, He has given us so much concerning marriages, parenting and how to rule our homes. He said, how can a man rule the house of God if he cannot rule his own home.

The culture of the kingdom is how we treat each other: loving each other, caring for each other, and being there for each other. Those virtues once they are cultivated in the home eventually will translate into the community. Even the church will benefit from those virtues in your home. When you have a good marriage and your children in subjection, it is translated into every other aspect of your life. The community will receive benefits, as well. The culture of God is being created in your home through his word. It spreads throughout the community where those virtues and morals then can be shared among other people. The whole purpose of creating a kingdom culture is to touch the lives of others.

I stated earlier, everything began in the garden. Just as Satan disrupted the culture in the garden, he has continued to disrupt the culture. But God through Jesus Christ has restored the kingdom. God has given us the authority through our kingship to restore the culture of his kingdom in our families and on the earth.

Satan was in the garden. He wanted to circumvent God's plan by creating his culture here on earth after his image.

In the garden, God wanted man to live through revelation, not experimentation. He put man in Eden to duplicate on the earth what it is in heaven. But because man disobeyed God, the culture of religion was created. Remember religion is nothing but a substitute for God's will and presence. But thanks be to God who gives us victory through Christ Jesus. He converted things back to His original plan. Today, God is raising a culture of believers to spread his love and His word in the earth.

The kingdom of God is a visible manifestation of a comprehension rule of God over every area of our lives. The kingdom culture is what we live by, it is ruled by truth. It is our job as believers to trust in God's Word and to trust His character. He will do what He says. We must be the agents of change that God will use to recreate the culture that he had from the beginning. It must begin as I stated earlier in our homes, churches, and communities. Jesus said, "Upon this rock, I will build my church and the gates of hell shall not prevail". As men in the kingdom we are to rule and govern our families in a way that brings glory to the King. We must be men of integrity. We must be examples of love and grace. We must be accountable to God and one another in the communities we serve. What does your family culture look like?

Reclaiming Your Kingship

Chapter Six

Walk with God

This world is desperate for godly people like you to enter their kingship as an image bearer of Christ. Jesus loves the world, and He has made provision for its restoration through you. You were born a winner. The whole world is waiting for you to exercise your God-given authority to act like a son of God. It's worth repeating, Romans 8:19 reads, for the creation waits in eager expectation for the children of God to be revealed.

We are to walk with God into our destiny. God created us for the enjoyment of an exclusive relationship with Him that involves companionship, intimacy, and dominion. God's grace continues to beckon us closer to Him.

We have a mandate to manifest the kingdom of God, right here and right now. Don't lay down your crown in defeat. You are a king because Jesus has made you king. God wants us in an intimate friendship with him. He wants us to walk it out through the course of our everyday lives. The goal we're after is an everyday walk of unbroken communion with our Lord and friend.

Enoch walked with God three hundred years, and begat sons and daughters. So all the days of Enoch were six hundred and sixty-five years. And *Enoch walked with God;* and he was not, for God took him (Genesis 5:22–24).

Just as Enoch walked with God, so are we to walk with him. As we draw closer to God, He will not likely take us up to heaven as He did Enoch. However, He does want to reveal his face to us. He will open the Scriptures to us through the spirit of wisdom and revelation and reveal to us the light of the glory of God that is to be found in him.

Maturity causes us to see ourselves the way God see us. It is the key to our manhood. Our manhood is developed in our walk with the Father. It is imperative that we are consistent in studying His word, prayer, and walking out His truths. We respond to life by applying His word. Consistency will break the things that try to hinder maturity. An immature king doesn't understand his power or his authority. He will be negligent in his responsibility to God and to his family. We must take this commission with great seriousness.

As God brings the restoration of all things to men, we are a very important part of that. When we journey with God, He unfolds the secrets of his kingdom. *"I will give you the keys of the kingdom of heaven, and whatever you bind on earth shall be bound in heaven, and whatever you loose on earth shall be loosed in heaven"* Matthews 16:19.

God gives us keys to unlock the mysteries of His kingdom. When we understand the mysteries of the kingdom we have access to His power to defeat the enemy. The scriptures say that we have power to tread upon serpents and scorpions and over ALL the power of the devil. Satan is no match for us. Let me say it like this, Satan is no match for *you*.

This is a great privilege of walking with our King. You have the freedom to move in victory.

There is a secret place where we develop a growing relationship with God. Hidden in the secret place, we learn how to become His friends, and we find out what pleases him. The inner chambers of our heart are primed for a life that is rooted and grounded in love. This secret place is often developed in private with God before he releases us publicly.

Noah was a just man, walked faithfully with God Genesis 6:9. Noah knew the secret of walking with God. This allowed him to have the ability to endure the suffering that can result with obeying God's voice. We can learn how to walk and obey God's voice in the secret place.

In Genesis 24:40, it reads, *And he said to me, 'The Lord, before whom I have walked, will send His angel with you to make your journey successful, and you will take a wife for my son from my relatives and from my father's house. Abraham's walk with God resulted in his position as the father of many nations. Our journey can be just as amazing if we surrender completely. Not only for us but our descendants as well.*

Through Christ, we can explore the glorious riches of knowing God like they did and to even a greater degree because of the Spirit which has been given to us.

God works with his friends. We are His friends when we walk closely with Him. The Father wants to use you. He wants to work with friends who are loyal to him. We prove ourselves as his friends through the trails of life, and how we response to situations and circumstances that arise.

> **God wants to walk with us before He works through us.**

^{14} Ye are my friends, if ye do whatsoever I command you.

^{15} Henceforth I call you not servants; for the servant knoweth not what his lord doeth: but I have called you friends; for all things that I have heard of my Father I have made known unto you.

^{16} Ye have not chosen me, but I have chosen you, and ordained you, that ye should go and bring forth fruit, and that your fruit should remain: that whatsoever ye shall ask of the Father in my name, he may give it you.

God has chosen us to walk closely with him. As we draw near to Him, He also draws near to us. As we embrace this position of friendship with God, we will know what to do in our marriages, on our jobs, and in every aspect of life. We are His friends.

Jesus told us that he confides his (his secrets) to his friends. Tell the Lord, you want to be His friend, His confidant, loyal to the death. Walk with Him, talk with Him, listen to Him, hear His heart, and take his hand and let Him lead you into your kingship. Teach me. Lord, to walk with you!

Reclaiming Your Kingship

Chapter Seven
Manhood, Marriage, and Ministry

As children, we were often told to "man up" or "act like a man". It's interesting because those who were giving the commands were speaking to our masculinity. They assumed that children could access their manhood just by being instructed to do so. We didn't even know what that meant. Most times, it meant be strong or don't cry. Show no weakness. But that is not what manhood is all about.

Our definition of manhood must come from the One who created man – God. Jesus modeled it. He was both God and man. He did cry *but* He is strong. He is both the lion and the lamb.

If any clarity is needed in defining manhood, we simply must look to the life of Jesus.

When we look at His example of manhood, we see love, integrity, honesty, wisdom, humility, selflessness, courage, provision, faithfulness, etc. Manhood encompasses all of these traits and more.

Manhood is lived out by following God's word. It never needs to be proven.

True kings walk boldly in their manhood in close proximity to the King. They reject fear and shame, and reflect the glory of the Father. They embrace the fact that they are created in the image and likeness of God.

When Adam and Eve were created, they were given the task to rule over the earth. (Genesis 1:26-28). Adam's task was to recognize who he was in God first. God put him in the garden and gave him commands. And the Lord God took the man and put him into the garden of Eden to dress it and to keep it. Genesis 2:15.

Adam's identity was in God. Ours, too. manhood *is always* connected to God.

When we have a full grasp of who we are as men, it spills over into how we treat our families. I have the honor of saying; my wife is my best friend and my partner in ministry. We walk out our life together by following

God's word. Our love and partnership bless our Father and exalts Him as King over our lives. This is how God intended it from the beginning, husbands and wives would operate as one, doing ministry together. As we partner together God is glorified.

When Mary was given the assignment to raise Jesus, Joseph came alongside her to carry out that purpose.

Aquila and Priscilla were a great example of a married couple faithfully working ministry together. These are examples God uses to show us how it should be done.

In ministering alongside your spouse, it is key to learn how to minister to each other. Besides your close connection to the King, your first and foremost ministry is to your wife.

This does not mean your ministry should only be to your marriage, but it should flow out of your marriage to the world. We have a responsibility to God to cultivate strong marriages and families. In order for our marriages to be strong, we must work on ourselves individually. We can only work on our marriages by working on ourselves.

An honorable king is one who recognizes his own strengths and weaknesses. He rightly identifies where he is spiritually, emotionally, and mentally and adjusts without getting stuck in pride. No human is strong in every area. We all have work to do on ourselves.

You must walk in humility and love with those you lead. This includes honoring your wife. Give her the level of respect that you want to receive. Allow room for her to operate in her gifts, talents, and abilities. Refuse to be intimidated by her gifts. You are one. Her gifts strengthen your team.

Offer your wife grace as you serve her. Show her love and respect. This will allow the two of you to flow together. Always keep your marriage and family ahead of your business and/or ministry.

Authentic manhood requires that a man groom his sons and daughters to operate in the kingdom, teaching them the ways of the Lord. He should be loving and kind. The Bible warns us to not provoke our children to anger. We should not rule with an iron hand.

Genesis 33:13-14 reads, *My lord knows that the children are weak, and the flocks and herds which are nursing are with me. And if the men should drive them hard one day, all the flock will die. Please let my lord go on ahead before his servant. I will lead on slowly at a pace which the livestock that go before me, and the children, are able to endure until I come to my lord in Seir."*

Sometimes in ministry, it can be easier and faster to do things alone, but God did not call you to go on your own. It is not good for man to be alone. Consider the pace of your wife and your children. You don't want to be going so fast in ministry that you lose everybody and end up at your destination alone.

Slow down the pace of your ministry to the pace of your marriage. It may be better to do less and have seemingly less "success" but do it with more people than to run so fast and lose your marriage, family, and your health in the process. Sometimes the pace and speed of our ministries can be extremely harmful to the health of our marriages.

There are areas we need to pay attention to going forward. They all come from our manhood. By recognizing these areas it will help us stay focused on the mission of serving Christ together.

Find your identity in Jesus, not in ministry.

If our primary identity is in doing ministry, instead of finding our joy, confidence, and fulfillment in Jesus, it will negatively impact your manhood, ministry and your marriage. We must be careful because this is the ploy of the evil one. Rule your household well with love.

Connect with your wife daily.

Let God be our primary motivation for your marriage. That means we must give attention to our wives, not neglecting them or exchanging evil for evil.

If you are a king, that makes your wife a queen. Treat her as such and she will respond in kind. God has called us together, let's look to shine as a team in God's kingdom.

Chapter Eight

Act Like a King

You are set as king in God's kingdom and no man can take that away from you. When you were born again you became a new creature in Christ Jesus and part of a priesthood of ruling citizens Christ could use to advance His reign. *"But ye are a chosen generation, a royal priesthood, a holy nation, a peculiar people; that ye should show forth the praises of him who hath called you out of darkness into his marvelous light"* (1 Peter 2:9). *"And ye shall be unto me a kingdom of priests and a holy nation"* (Exodus 19:6).

The word "kingdom" means dominion, reign, realm, kingdom, and sovereignty.

The same word is closely related to the Greek word malak meaning to be king and ruler, to make king and ruler, or to become king and ruler.

You are a king/priest destined to reign. We reign with our King (Rev 5:10) and we shall *reign on the earth*. We are to reign now. The Greek word for 'reign' is '*basileuoo*' which means to have kingly rule, to possess kingly dominion, to exercise kingly power.

How is it then, that having been predestined to reign and rule in this life, we are still broken by the situations we are facing in life?

Is it possible that this is due to the fact that we have been ignorant of our position in Christ?

Grace has elevated us to a position of rulership in life; it is now time to live in that reality, daily.

We are God's vessels of honor here on earth. So let's live out our kingship by embracing who we were created to be.

Reigning is very different from escaping. It's evident in scripture that Christ never intended to save us so we could escape this world. In fact, He saved us so we could overcome the world.

"For whatsoever is born of God overcometh the world: and this is the victory that overcometh the world, even our faith" 1 John 5:4.

Many believe that Jesus is the Christ, but never do anything to make a difference with their lives. You are not like that. You are God's chosen. You are a king and a priest advancing Christ's kingly reign.

Your ministry is not yet finished. There is still much to do. The King wants you to be innocent as lambs in your treatment of others. That requires that you walk in maturity. Maturity does not come with age but with accepting responsibility. As we grow as men, we have to take full responsibility for our lives and that of our families.

That is a sign of your kingship, a king accepts responsibility. After Adam sinned, he blamed his wife by saying *the woman you gave me caused me to eat.*

As a king growing in our manhood, we must hate and reject passivity. Passive behavior is what got Adam in trouble. He did not rebuke the enemy when he came for his wife. We shouldn't sit idly by and watch the world go by. God has not created us to be passive men. It causes us to be spiritually impotent.

When we are passive we go along to get along. *What we allow, we must eventually tolerate.*

So, let's make a declaration today:

I reject passivity in my life today. I recognize that refusing to act results in failure. I refuse to fail. I choose to act on the word of God. I choose to take an active lead in my life and that of my family. God has given me the spirit of power, love and a sound mind.

I am a man of decisive action directed by the Holy Spirit. I am the king, He created me to be. Passivity will not stop my determination to accept my kingship.

I am a man that will continue to grow in my masculinity. Masculinity doesn't mean that I will never mess up, but that I am seeking to be more transparent and honest by correcting errors and owning mistakes. I commit to being honest with myself, honest with God and honest with my wife.

As kings, our potential and power are wasted when we carry secrets of unconfessed and unrepentant sins. If we knew how powerful we were as kings, we would deal with those secrets and would not carry around such things in our hearts.

The thing about secrets is they will eventually come to light. So it is important that we find someone that we trust to share with. Shine the light on your sin. Darkness is where the devil lives.

He is an expert maneuvering through darkness. As we expose sin, light comes and maturity is developed. So don't be afraid to expose the works of darkness that may be hindering your growth.

1 Corinthians 16:13 reads, *"Be on the alert, Stand firm in the faith, Act like men (kings) Be strong."*

These are four commands that God gives us to help us mature in our kingship. Let's break each one down.

Be on the alert: This speaks of being aware of the enemy. Know where the devil is at all times. Not only in your life but the life of your family. Recognize the enemy when he's trying to come against your marriage, children, finances, career and every area of your life. This is a spiritual battle, and the devil is trying to lull you to sleep. Stay awake at all times.

Keep your guard up through prayer. Remember you are the king; your family depends on you being alert and aware of the enemy at all times.

Stand firm in your faith: Don't let go of your confidence in God and his word. Be confident and bold in your faith, don't be intimidated by the devil.

Don't waver. Be sure of God and what He is able to do for and through you. Don't doubt His power. Don't ever give up.

The lion is courageous as king of the jungle. It is in his identity and authority that he rules. He is intimidated by none. There is no fear in the heart of the lion/king.

I John 4:8 says, *there is no fear in love, perfect love casteth out fear.* There is no fear in the lion's heart. His fearlessness is heard in the power of his roar.

The roar is the communication line of the lions. When the male roars it strikes fear in the heart of those around him. There is a blessing in our roar as men of God.

Ecclesiastes 8:4 *For the words of a king is authority and power and who can say to him, what are you doing?*

When we function in our authority it should strike fear in the heart of Satan and his cohorts. The devil should know us by name. Just as he knew Jesus and Paul.

As born-again believers we have that kind of power, and we can walk in it. We have access to glory in the Holy Spirit. God will manifest His glory through us.

Every truly born-again believer has access to this kingship through an authentic relationship with the Lord. As we roar over

our families as kings and walk in our kingship, we will begin to see the fullness of our destiny.

Act like men: We are men of God created to lead. Paul is summoning us to be courageous and brave. We will face opposition in life. Yet, stand up in your manhood. There may be

dangerous situations to confront. Do it in courage knowing that God is on your side.

Stand in the gap for your wives and children. Nehemiah 4:14 *Be not afraid of them remember the Lord which is great and terrible and fight for your brethren, your son, and your daughter, your wives and your houses.*

As we remember the Lord He becomes our shield and are able to act like the men God has called us to be. We will love our wives and raise our children in the fear of the Lord. As men we will guard our territory against the enemy and pursue our Lord with relentless passion.

Be strong. This is not a physical command but a spiritual one. Strength comes through our consistency in Christ. It drives us to seek God for our everyday routine.

'Be strong' means do not compromise your walk with God. Resist temptation and live upright before Him. Although it may sound odd, you can be strong and still have weaknesses. Strength is demonstrated when you admit your weakness and forsake your sin.

Being strong is knowing how you will respond to situations before they happen. As kings, let's believe what God has said about us. God is our strength.

It helps bring security to your family. Your wife won't have to worry about your character. The Alpha male is consistent in protecting his pride. He won't back down or change his behavior when a challenge occurs.

Just as the male and female lion work in harmony to lead the pride, so must men and women of God. God designed us a team. And what a dynamic team we are! We don't need to be intimidated by the gifts, talents, and abilities of others.

The lion knows that his lioness is a far better hunter than himself. He understands how she is an advantage to their team. He gets to eat more zebra and elephant steaks. He is not at all threatened by her strengths because he is certain about who he is and who God created him to be. Her gifts make his team stronger. And His gifts make her feel more secure. Everyone is moving in their purposes, doing what God created them to do.

Chapter Nine

Satan: Identity Thief

Satan is a crook. You know that he kills, steals, and destroys. But know this, that one of the most valuable things he is after is your identity. You can't defeat him without it. A loss of identity is like kryptonite. It leaves you powerless.

Satan will not ever *stop* coming for you and your family. He hates that you are created in the image of likeness of God. He hates that you love God and your family, and that you have power over him.

Genesis 1:27 *So God created man in his own image, in the image of God created he him; male and female created he them.*

God created us to look like Him and to act like Him. But Satan wants you to look and act like him. The battle has been raging since the beginning of time. Today, Satan is still trying to look like God through mankind. But in

Colossians we see what Jesus did for us. Colossian 1:15-16 *Who is the image of the invisible God, the firstborn of every creature: For by him were all things created, that are in heaven, and that are in earth, visible and invisible, whether they be thrones, or dominions, or principalities, or powers: all things were created by him, and for him:*

Jesus is the image of God. He was able to bring the kingdom of God to earth. Jesus became the second Adam. First Corinthians 15:44- 45 the first Adam was made a living soul, the last Adam was made a quickening spirit. Jesus connected us to God. Christ in you that's the hope of glory. That's why the battle is so great. Because if you never recognize who you are in the kingdom of God, Satan will always have the upper hand.

There is a principle, whatever God converts, Satan perverts. Satan wants to be God and rule over your life. The desires of Satan are listed in Isaiah 14:12-14.

For thou hast said in thine heart, I will ascend into heaven, I will exalt my throne above the stars of God: I will sit also upon the mount of the congregation, in the sides of the north: I will ascend above the heights of the clouds; I will be like the Most High.

Satan's "I wills" are indicators of the pride that got him kicked out of heaven. Still he has been trying to be like

God. He is nothing but a cheap counterfeit. In him, the spirit of religion originated. Satan used what God said and turned it inside out. It is the same strategy he uses today.

The "I wills" of Satan are perverse. His declarations can be summed up in one-word *pride.* It comes in many forms: arrogance, self-righteousness, boasting, self-sufficiency, deceitfulness, selfishness, people-pleasing, etc. The list is long. We have to watch out for pride lest we find ourselves living in it.

When we refuse to yield to anyone, put our desires above our families, seek power and position, try to impress people, we succumb to pride. It is a crafty spirit. We must pray for a heart of humility. Pride is the downfall of many men. God resists the proud but gives grace to the humble (James 4:6).

Satan wants to sabotage and undermine man's self-worth. He wants to get rid of God's rule and authority over man.

Remember Satan is a thief and a liar. But the King's word is law and truth. Satan wants to pervert the word to undermine the authority of the King.

> *The spirit of religion says let's keep God's word, but get rid of him as our authority.*

In religion, we can learn about God but not about His kingdom. We learn the law, the rituals, the sacraments, and the things of God. We apply them to the service of God without really knowing Him intimately.

The religious do not understand or receive the kingdom of God. They have a limited and distorted understanding of God's word.

God has given us a remedy through His son, Jesus Christ who is the King of all kings. As we pursue the King and learn to live within His kingdom, our purpose will become clearer.

We will walk in our full authority and influence. We will provoke our wives and children to do the same. We will influence our communities, our cities, and our nations. Because that's what kings do.

www.ingramcontent.com/pod-product-compliance
Lightning Source LLC
Chambersburg PA
CBHW051707090426
42736CB00013B/2586